Towards a Doctrine
of
Creative Education

*

essay

*

Traumear

Paperback ISBN 978-0-244-32058-4

*

www.traumear.com

*

All creativity that is live and not merely mechanical has to begin with the creator's inward awareness of himself and must pass from there to an increasing practical knowledge by him of how his reactions to the reluctance of the material to be shaped can be transformed by him into responsible actions which will, with sufficient practical application, in good time, turn into spontaneous behaviour. In that sense we can then speak of creative teaching and educating.

*

Towards a Doctrine
of
Creative Education

When we say that a child 'wants to be educated' we mean something very specific. Obviously no child wants to sit at a desk for hours each day for reasons he cannot understand. Neither does he particularly seek the company of the same adult frequently so as to acquire what that adult makes available to him. If we say that a child actually wants to be educated we mean something like a drive in that child, towards an unknown quantity, or something like a desire, or a longing, or an urge - in a direction not yet to be recognized by the child.

And really that 'want' to be educated begins at birth. How could it be otherwise? A human being is a peculiar being. It is born in one state and wants to march on to another. All other beings remain in the same state. As they are born, so they remain, and some of them go to great lengths to remain as they were born. We observe that and marvel. We call it survival. The laws of survival are as wide open to comprehension as the men who invent them. They deal, however, with a single-state life-form. The laws of survival deal with single-state beings in such a way that these beings may remain forever open to human intervention. This openness to human interest and human care has to be discovered yet as the mainspring of these single-state, lawful beings. All beings except human beings, that-is to say: everything in heaven and on earth that is not a human being, has a side or an aspect to it, by law, from which it may quite naturally be approached by human beings and – learned.

What does it mean, then, to learn something? It means to unite with something in such a way that its lawful susceptibility to human influence becomes plain.

This is of course another way of saying that all things and beings are created for human beings. If we ask: How are they, under the law of survival, created for human beings? – then the answer is: So that they may be learned.

*

A human being is born in one state and must be raised into another state. This is not a matter of survival, however, but an actual fact of life. The one fact, that it wants to rise into that second state, and the other fact, that it must be raised into that second state, are really one and the same truth. A single insight comprehends them both.

There is the state of survival and there is the state of life. The latter is not lawful but free. When we say 'free', we do not mean lawless. Far from it. What we mean is a state of being in which human beings interact without recourse to laws. Laws were like the ladder which was climbed to achieve that second state', the state of life.

Who are teachers? They are human beings in the second state of being who wish to raise children to that same second state. They know that all human beings want to be raised to that state of freedom out of a state of lawfulness and they realize that no human being can do that entirely under his or her own steam. At the same time they experience a distinct longing in themselves to lend a hand, in fact to lend the necessary hand, so that survival may be crowned by life, lawfulness by freedom.

*

This longing is given to teachers in the state of life. We are born into survival and reborn into life. The desire to teach comes to teachers along with their rebirth. I mean creative teaching here, not a standard variety. We are interested in the whole human being here, not only in the forty-nine percent that survive. A whole human being, in that sense, is born and re-

2

born. Someone who remains in the state of survival is not a whole human being. Someone who for a long time experiences the desire to be free of the law but is not given the necessary helping hand to attain to that freedom begins to lose courage, and instead of the freedom, he espouses the laws of survival. In that case he lowers himself beneath all beings, because he is no longer open to the influence of human beings. No being in heaven or on earth is able actually to espouse the laws of survival except the human being. When a human being does that he is to be pitied, because he "knows not what he does". Education cannot reach him. He is unteachable. He will not learn. If we use the words 'teaching' and 'learning' to describe the raising and rising, respectively, from the first state of being to the second state, then clearly where an insistence upon the first state is the case, neither of these can go on. Where someone does not any longer wish to learn and to be educated, he is clearly no longer a real human being and falls into a category. Human being is not a category, but he falls into a category. We pity him. If only he had been given a helping hand when the time was ripe!

*

When we speak of a born teacher we should really mean someone who is 'reborn' with the desire to educate. While still in a state of survival, a human being obviously cannot raise anyone into the state of freedom. What he will do is 'teach' survival tactics, which effort must always imply the impression that survival will do, will suffice, for human beings. Survival tactics – and there is such a thing – cannot, however, be in fact learned and taught; they can only be picked up by experience, in the school of necessity. A curriculum of survival tactics is like an encouragement to learn how to breathe, to eat, or to sleep, and to call that education. Of course a truly wonderful complication can be caused here, which has been done, so that these laws of survival and the tactics of survival have practically taken over in men's bodies and minds, to the veritable exclusion of life and freedom. Anyone who speaks of an education to life and freedom is therefore viewed as a fool or as an upstart, however speak of it we shall.

*

The desire to be educated and to be free may at first be a blind, unconscious one, so that part of the teacher's task is the raising of this urge to a conscious awareness. When someone is able to say: "Yes, I do want to learn and, come to think of it, I have probably always wanted to learn," he has progressed from when he was not yet aware that he wanted to learn. The same, however, can be said for a teacher. Someone may always have wanted to teach, though he only recently became aware of it. However, learning and teaching are not, so to speak, equidistant from the human centre. All want to learn, whether they know it or not, but not all want to teach. Only a few want to teach. It would help if we asked for more teachers.

I mention the desire to learn and the urge to teach in the same breath because both must be brought to the awareness, and because both require attention in order to flourish. Also, when we compare these two longings, we learn a great deal about each. The wish to learn, for example, is with us from birth and leads towards maturity, whereupon it continues in one form or another. The urge to teach cannot come upon us until maturity. The person who says that he has been wanting to teach since he was four must therefore be talking about something else, such as the passing on of survival tactics. In an important sense, the urge to teach could be described as the desire to pass on the experience of maturity.

Maturity, therefore, is a critical point of departure for a teacher. What he means by maturity is worth looking at. We mentioned that it means freedom, especially freedom from standards and laws. The experience of this freedom, which can be called another birth, such as a birth of fire or spirit, in comparison to a birth by nature or water, puts us into a unique position from which to contemplate one another and the world, and teachers take it upon themselves to make this experience attractive, to make this freedom attainable and acceptable to those who are not yet mature. This is no altruistic bias on their part but they decide they cannot themselves contain or possess this freedom unless they hold it out to others. Thank god there are some teachers.

Maturity allocates the human centre of learning in the individual person. Prior to that, this centre was by necessity located in a teacher-pupil relationship. A teacher, because he is an adult, can learn by paying attention to his own inner motions and commotions. A child can not. He can do a great deal by attending in that way, but he cannot learn. In order to learn in the sense in which we mean it here, a child must be drawn into a relationship with a teacher. Meanwhile that teacher knows of course that this human centre of learning exists authentically within himself, and that by drawing the child into a relationship with himself he extends that centre of learning, that human awareness of inward motion and commotion, to the learning child.

We may go on to inquire then what this centre of learning amounts to. It certainly has nothing to do with survival but everything with freedom and life. But big words are cheap. A mature centre of learning is first of all the possession of a certain knowledge; something we know cannot be taken away from us. What this knowledge is, varies from one mature person to the next. The fact that it exists and is possessed by someone makes for his maturity.

How do we come to possess certain knowledge? The answer is: sufficient learning. When is learning sufficient? As soon as such knowledge sets in. Thereafter we learn in a different fashion. What is the nature of certain knowledge and how can we describe it? It may be applied without diminishment. It may be contemplated without application. It may be relied upon without contemplation. These might be called the three tests of certain knowledge.

*

The reverse, of course, is equally true. As we rely on this knowledge, we may contemplate it and apply it, all three at the same time, if we wish, or separately, or two at a time.

Only those who have certain knowledge can talk about it, as I do at the moment, for example, but those who do not have it, when they hear about it, their appetite may well be aroused. Then begins their striving for certain knowledge, because certainty is powerful. It allows us to hold out in the face of evil.

I cannot really be a teacher until I have certain knowledge, that should go without saying. And yet there are many who hold the position of teachers and in everything they know they are uncertain. Within themselves they are without authority and without authenticity. One would like to remind them of the need to learn before teaching. Their teaching is a broadcasting of opinion and a multiplication of prejudice.

A reliance on certain knowledge is primary. We do not depend on others to agree with us, because we rest secure in our own ability to make sensible decisions and to arrive at satisfactory conclusions. We recognize uncertainty in others and we know how to respond to it. Our compassion with the uncertainty of others is responsible. We are not afraid of being shaken in our certainty, but on the contrary, we look forward to it, since we know that in our own sensitivity to the uncertainty of others lies the key to their hearts.

Our complete reliance on our own certain knowledge, then, allows us to be sensitive to the uncertainty of others. We do well, therefore, to learn how to rely on this knowledge. Let's begin by admitting that it must be inward, not outward. If it were outward we would be able to point to it and some sign of it would be available. However no sign of it can exist. Those who demand a sign before they accept such knowledge can never be certain. The inwardness of certain knowledge however makes it readily available to us quite independently of circumstances. Conditions do not need to be right for it. Even as I rely upon it myself at this moment I am not affected by what goes on around me.

So we may take this for granted, that due to our reliance on certain inward knowledge we are not any more swayed to our detriment by circumstances. In addition, the way we rest within the still centre of our human being is a sensible and satisfactory contribution to our environment. Whatever goes on around us benefits from it. And the greatest benefit is gained by those who find themselves enabled, in our company, to confess their uncertainty. This is not necessarily a matter of asking questions. What counts is that someone admits his uncertainty to himself. This amounts to an activation of the learning centre. If in your presence I am able to come to terms with some aspect of my insecurity or with some part of my insufficiency, then you have rendered me a great service. However, not until you, in my presence, relied on your certain inward knowledge did it occur to me that there was room in me for definite gain.

So we must keep in mind here that this reliance is not a mere mechanical habit or pretentious routine but a definite gain. As I, with all my weaknesses and shortcomings and incapacities drew near to you, you were shaken, to some extent, in your inward and knowledgeable certainty, it could not be otherwise. This knowledge is not a defense behind which you hide, but a resource which you like to make available to others. And you do make it available by relying on it in the face of their uncertainty.

*

How easy this is to say – and how difficult to do! Even once we know with a certainty what resources of, say, forgiveness and understanding reside in us, we still get bowled over and hatred is inflamed in us. It seems such a contradiction! However first the demand, then the supply; that is the rule in the life of action. And an educator is a man or woman of action. First the pupil must be given the opportunity to demonstrate, at least to himself, his ignorance. The teacher knows that this ignorance is relative to the resources available. In the presence of the teacher with greater resources, more ignorance is liable to manifest itself in the pupil. We should never suppose, therefore, that the so-called 'good' teacher is the one who meets with no resistance from pupils, or that the best teacher has the least resistance to confront. The opposite is the case. On one hand the demand for knowledge never exceeds the availability, on the other hand it initially manifests itself as resistance to the teacher. This is how the teacher experiences it. The pupil, on the other hand, 'experiences' this initially as nothing more articulate than pressure. He cannot help but demonstrate this pressure to the teacher. But the teacher experiences a resistance of himself, and is therefore tempted to condemn the pupil as ignorant. The better teacher is then the one who interprets this resistance, more correctly, as the pupil's unconscious and unavoidable 'mere' reaction to his own, the teacher's, resource for knowledge.

We can simplify this even further by pointing to the teacher as the <u>source</u> of knowledge, and the teacher knows himself as a source of knowledge, and as soon as he experiences pupil resistance and is therefore unavoidably somewhat shaken in his security, he reaches for his certain knowledge as a <u>resource</u>.

So the resistance the teacher experiences in the pupil is a manifest demand for knowledge. It is such a demand, even though the pupil can hardly be given the credit for it. From the point of view of the pupil there is pressure and nothing but pressure.

How can the pupil be brought, by the teacher, to the point where he accepts the responsibility for this pressure? Certainly the pupil has no resources. The onus is definitely on the teacher. Unless the teacher is careful, the pupil will feel this pressure mount in him and then either react to it or reject it. What a shame if he rejects it, which he does by at least inwardly turning away from the teacher and ignoring him. "I want nothing to do with this pressure, nor with you as a teacher," says the pupil then, and that particular opportunity for education is lost. Or, how horrible if the pupil reacts to the pressure! He accuses the teacher of intending harm and blames him for causing him discomfort. "I hate you," says the pupil, "and I hate what you are trying to do to me. You have no right to put me under all this pressure." One misconception leads to the next. There is attack and counter-attack. The charge of unkindness is met by the counter-charge of laziness, against which the accusation of injustice is levied, and finally the teacher stands there as the self-appointed tyrant and the pupil is the terrorist.

And where the pupil rejects the pressure and the teacher, the teacher is liable to become ineffectual by saying: "I refuse to accuse you of insolence. You reject me, but I will tolerate you. You have started to lie to me, so I will collude with you and lie back to you. You hide from me your capacity as a pupil, so I will hide from you my potency as a teacher. Let's be mates. As long as you pretend to go along with my instructions and while you pay lip-service to my office as a teacher, I will not treat you harshly and will even like you. You may even become my favourite."

So what shall we say? On one side the tyrant, on the other the – hypocrite? How can the teacher navigate between this Scylla and Charybdis? How can he overcome cowardice on one side and self-righteousness on the other? He steers to one side, for comfort and relief from the whirlpool and the attack, only to run the risk of being sucked into immoral ineffectuality. He is horrified by the lack of discipline and ambition, by the laziness and laissez-faire attitude, so he exerts himself, forces the issue, artificially raises his self-esteem at the expense of pupil-character and runs the risk of turning into a harmful mechanical force.

At the inner still centre of his being, let the teacher therefore seek to locate the resistance of the pupil, and then he will endeavour to identify it correctly as a sign of the pupil's learning capacity rather than as unwillingness. He will acknowledge to himself that the pupil cannot possibly be charged with conscious, intentional resistance of the teacher since the pupil is unaware of anything except pressure from within himself, where certain quantities are coming forward in response to the teacher's certain knowledge. The teacher knows, meanwhile, that the pupil cannot really learn until he takes the responsibility, somehow, for these inner urges. Telling the pupil to do so, in so many words, is useless, since the pupil sees things - cannot but see things – differently. And all this time the teacher experiences resistance which he, in his capacity as teacher, correctly 'solves' as the pressure the pupil 'experiences'.

Still the crucial act has not been performed by the teacher. Two indispensable preliminary steps have been taken by him, along the path of active education. We should not tire of stressing the importance of these. The teacher experiences something as resistance in the pupil. That comes at the start. If a teacher is already so far gone on the wide road of cowardice or self-righteousness, of mateyness or overbearance, that he cannot experience any such resistance, he has to return to basics, and would be wise to do so as soon as possible. Even in his own within-self must the teacher be open and alert to this experience of resistance. After all he does bring something entirely new to the pupil – if he really is a teacher[1] – and in the face of the new there is always a resistance, one can take that for granted. Let the teacher, therefore, at the beginning, bring forward what he has to offer until he meets with this resistance. He does not try to avoid it, during this first preliminary step, nor does he somehow try to bring it about. It comes from the pupil. And it is not anger in the teacher, or haste, or reluctance, or ambition, in *reaction* to which this specific pressure in the pupil arises but it is the still centre of the teacher's being which the pupil *resists*. The teacher waits for it, is alert to it, is wide awake in anticipation of it. He would be smart to practice with individual pupils too, in order to become more and more acute, more sharp and sensitive, more alert and intelligent – in anticipation of this resistance; for come it will, if he is indeed offering something worthwhile, something new and real to the pupil. Of crucial importance is the fact that this resistance must arise when the teacher least expects it, when he is not looking; that it will sneak in, so to speak, "like a thief in the night". On the other hand he realizes that he must not bar his gate or bolt his door. After all, he desires to educate that individual child, so he will welcome any sign of individuality, on which he can then build and which he can follow up. How silly of the teacher to wish for eternally calm seas! He needs a breeze. A nice stiff breeze allows him to put his navigation skills into practice – allows him to educate. The entirely 'willing pupil', The one most cooperative and obedient, is not necessarily the one being most successfully educated. Is the teacher being lulled into unawareness? Is he falling asleep, on account of so much pleasant progress? Let him be especially on his guard. Perhaps nothing worthwhile is going on. Perhaps no education is taking place. Then, suddenly, a resistance surprises him, overwhelms him, and – he becomes fearful or hateful. He becomes critical. He

---

[1] – and not merely a functionary hired by the state to prepare pupils for employment.

feels betrayed etc. etc.

This preliminary step: – the more we look at it, the more we understand the importance of it, at the very beginning of the education process.

Let's by all means, then, continue to speak of a resistance. It may appear, to the teacher, active or passive. The pupil may demonstrate reluctance or unwillingness in his manner and demeanor, he may show obstinacy and unruliness, he may state his unwillingness outright. Refractory behaviour, insubordination, petulance – all may be seen clearly in the light of the teacher's wise awareness as passive or active *resistance of the new, of the more real.*

What is it the teacher does now, when he says: "Here we do not have a case of this pupil consciously and intentionally pushing me and my source of knowledge away, of turning away from my knowledge for this or that reason previously thought about by him, but something else is actually going on, and I, as the teacher, have to transform what seems to me to be the case into what actually is the case, which is the following. The pupil is under pressure and I can see that. How do I know that the pupil is under pressure? I experience this resistance. What I experience as resistance, as myself and my knowledge being resisted, is in truth this pupil being under pressure. I choose to perform the creative act of correctly identifying that which at first seems to me to be something else. What I seem clearly to sense as resistance to me is in fact the pupil dimly sensing pressure on himself. As soon as I manage this interpretation I cannot help but welcome what I sense, because it guarantees me the real beginning of an individual education process.

I am glad that this has come about, although initially I flinched. I cannot expect of this pupil a similar act of interpretation vis-à-vis the pressure he senses. After all, he is the one in need of education, while I am the one who offers the education."

So the teacher is now glad that the pupil has evidently been contacted, been touched, by what he, the teacher, has put forward. This gladness also deserves special mention. It is itself *a creative act*, based on insight and stemming from knowledge; it is not a mere reflex. It is not the gladness of: "At last the difficulty has eased, the pain has stopped," but the gladness of: "At last I may begin to function more creatively, to engage with this pupil instructively!"

And now comes the crucial bit. The teacher actually lets the pupil see that he, the teacher, knows this pressure is being senses by the pupil and that he does not hold it against him, as though it were intentional resistance, but he feels compassion. The teacher chooses to feel compassion for the pupil under pressure and lets the pupil sense that.

*

Earlier we asked: How can the pupil be brought, or encouraged, by the teacher, to accept responsibility for the pressure he senses? It's clear that the pupil does not initially recognize the pressure as such, as something he can identify and deal with. How many people even over the age of thirty can do that? Usually one feels miserable and complains, or one bulldozes ahead in spite of the pressure, which amounts to the same, in that no real growth or creativity takes place.

A teacher must know how to deal with pressure in his own existence. There is spiritual pressure, psychic pressure, physical and carnal pressure. The teacher can identify it, as unique experience in every case, because he relates and refers it to the still inner centre of his being where, among other things, he has certain knowledge. He endeavours to identify any pressure that comes along as soon as possible, before it becomes too intense, and, most important, he says yes to it. This is his own individual creative act. He does not say no, but yes, to pressure. When it becomes too much for him to accept, he excuses himself in some way, but never without honestly admitting defeat. To admit defeat is an honourable thing. To pretend that one is not defeated when one has been is dishonourable.

One does not have to be a teacher in order to accept pressure as an opportunity for learning, but one can certainly not be a teacher if one is in the habit of either lying down under it or else riding roughshod over it. Some people react vehemently and forcefully in the face of pressure. Any pressure becomes for them a challenge to energetic behaviour, so that appearances are altered by them at a great rate but they themselves are not changed one jot. Such people say they enjoy being under pressure because – they like to press back. It amounts to that, to a resistance of pressure. Fate presses them, they in turn press their environment. The energy they exert on those around them they derive from the pressure they experience on themselves.

This is not what we mean by saying yes to pressure.

Those who lie down under pressure and learn somehow to tolerate it are not any better off. It is all the same, whether we complain or bully, if nothing substantial gets done. We can be spiritual, psychic, mental or carnal bullies or pulers.

*

The pressure experienced by a pupil is bound to be unique, because by a pupil we generally mean someone who is subjected to an education and, hopefully, submits to an education – that is formal. This word 'formal' is going to vex us for a time. Because quite justifiably the question arises as to what, after all, is the difference between the education to which every immature adult is subjected, to which every mature adult submits, and the education that can go on or is intended to go on in classrooms. A mature adult learns and it would not occur to him to cease from learning, while an immature adult can readily be seen to be under constraint to learn. In fact, when we

14

search among adults and compare the mature with the immature, we cannot do much better than to see the former as willing learners and the latter as reluctant ones.

Now what is generally meant by 'formal' education stands out for all to see, in terms of schoolhouses, hired teachers and examination papers, as a craft and even as an art. There is also such a thing as formal adult education, in many countries, where adults go back to school and submit themselves, for one reason or another, to formal education. Perhaps they reflect that when they were children, although they were subjected to formal education, either it didn't amount to much or they never got around to submitting to it, probably both, and now they intend to catch this up.

Evidently we have to take care with our terms here. Clearly education can be discussed as specifically the human process of learning and teaching within the context of our existence as individual and communal beings on earth. A doctrine of education has to begin from, and perhaps to return to, such a larger, more specific consideration of what it means to be drawn out of a lesser state by being introduced to a greater state. Formal education in particular can then be more genially pursued, both in the study and in the doing of it, as something like the play within the play; as something like the laboratory in comparison to ordinary experience; or, again, as something like an art within the context of reality. If we condescend now to speak of the play within the play, of the laboratory and the art, as formal, in comparison to its greater setting, then we find ourselves searching for a word to describe the non-formal, to which we compare the formal. We could, for example, make the distinction in terms of just plain education and formal education, always remaining mindful of that important factor which is frequently neglected, namely, that the greater includes and embraces the lesser, and that the lesser exists to serve the greater in this sense. Art exists for life, not life for art. No healthy soul desires to remain in the laboratory but it wishes to come out of it, upon having benefited. And of course the view, both conventional and superficial, of school-education is as of a means towards an end that lies outside of it.

However if by 'education' we always meant that greater process, which included formal or school education, we would soon be misunderstood, since convention and the fashion of our time does after all mean, by education, school education, or formal education.

All the same we feel that a doctrine of education is required which views education formal and education non-formal both, side by side, in comparison, and then in a working relation, the former within the latter, as a preparation towards it and as a creative instance or example of it.

*

This is not a doctrine of education but an essay towards such a doctrine, so we intend to look at the thing that interests us in several ways, as unbiased as possible, and always open to fresh insights and new approaches.

It seems to be easy to imagine a parent who observes his four year old offspring struggling with shoe laces and then the adult bends down and 'shows him how to do it'. "Do it like this," he says, meaning: "I know a way that works and if you imitate that way you will somehow be better off, perhaps, than if you wait until you have figured out your own way." He means 'perhaps' because he respects the child's individuality and because he knows that we all like to impress the world in our own way. He also realizes that most of us are clever at some activities and not so clever at others, and he understands that this is probably a providential arrangement, because it encourages togetherness and interdependence, and makes us less likely to neglect our higher, communal reality. – All this on account of the shoelaces. (Our parent is evidently of a philosophic disposition.)

That 'perhaps' is important. It strikes the tonic note of a melody in favour of education without coercion. Is such a thing possible? If the son of man must be raised, then surely that 'must' implies coercion, implies a 'thou shalt', and no buts about it. Sit down at your desk and get on with it, or else. Of course the 'or else' becomes problematic when for one reason or another the poor pedagogue is by law not any more allowed to smack the little backward beggar in the earhole. He has to become inventive now, with his 'or elses'. If he says to his pupil: "Do things my way or out you go!" he is liable to get a large look full of mixed feelings. Where school education is from the outset and by definition coercive, even punitive, dismissal sounds more like a promise than a threat.

Coercive formal education coincides with a particular attitude towards life. Those in favour of it mean well. They really suppose that by pushing children around they can turn them into better people. What usually happens is that children get used to being pushed around and then, in later life, they push others around. The bully is the natural product of this applied system. Nothing more tragically amusing than to witness an anti-bullying campaign in a school by teachers dedicated to coercive formal education. The caged cat bites off its claws.

But children who are bullied become better only in that they become like their elders, which is not always an unquestionable improvement. Bullies beget more bullies, which satisfies them. Then the sickness of self-analysis sets in. In some schools, if a male teacher stands behind a female pupil and touches her on the head or shoulder, he may be formally accused of sexual abuse. This clarifies the nature of bullying somewhat but only insofar as the symptoms have become complicated. No remedy is in sight

Coercive education is also Mephistophelian. One hears the gleeful spectre in the background, as he describes the modern man: "He shall eat dirt, and with relish!" (Mephisto in J.W.Goethe's 'Faust') A view of man as an arrogant upstart would seem to justify such an attitude. While we picture the natural man as overbearing proud, we just as naturally tend to take delight in breaking his spirit, which seems at the time like a convenient substitute for having our own broken, not to mention the consolation for already having had it broken.

So we're on dangerous ground here, with this business of: "You'll do as I say and like it!" After a while we give in and say: "You'll do as I say and pretend to like it!" So we end up with hypocrites in addition to the spiritual cripples. Some teachers become more likeable by saying: "Please do as I say, because I too am doing as I'm told," thus producing a generation of slaves. The coercion still exists, in spite of the castration. Others become sincere devils in the classroom. Liberated individuals bemoan their lack of freedom or create mischief in a spirit of revenge. Pupils become victims and accomplices. The effect of the 'teacher' in the classroom is like self-duplication. However there is hope for those who fall behind, for the 'problem pupils', for those who require remedial attention.

During the course of coercive education, therefore, the only hope that exists is for the drop-outs. A sobering reflection – and of course not at all acceptable by any appreciable slice of a civilized population.

*

If the natural man <u>must</u> be brought out of his confinement (which confinement can be discussed), and if children <u>must</u> be educated – and if all men, women and children <u>must</u> sooner or later come face to face with the spirit that is good – then we do well to have a close look at this 'must' before we jump to any conclusions, out of a false sense of self-perfection and other-direction.

If there is something here that is not to be avoided, something like the lawful essence of life, something that resides at the very centre of human growth, then this is the time for coming to terms with it. Even a few terms would do. Unless man is born of water *and* of spirit, he has neither the right to call himself human nor the privilege to be human.

As I write these words, for example, I come to the end of my tether. I have the choice now to look towards the good, so that it should inform me, and you through me – or else to become enamoured with my little patch of well-trodden, already over-grazed ground. The fact that I <u>interpret</u> this experience of being 'at the end of my tether', rather than accepting it at face value, is a creative act, voluntarily undertaken in open acknowledgment of the actual reality of what I mean by human growth, by human development and evolution. Such creative acts undertaken regularly by myself enable me to write with authority about education formal and non-formal. Any teacher in a classroom derives his own effective authority from no other source except this: that he interprets his disappointments, frustrations and setbacks in the light of an over-all vision of human growth. If human development and evolution in relation to the good is an empty phrase for him he has no business in a classroom or as a leader of others.

So we have to distinguish between the pressure, the forceful pressure, that is willfully or reluctantly applied by a would-be teacher, and the pressure that is incidentally experienced, or noticed on himself, by a pupil in the presence of an actual teacher.

*

When the pupil is under pressure, this is something that happens to him, and if he is comparatively inexperienced he will not even know he is under pressure but he will just feel miserable or awkward. To be able to say: "I am under pressure", this presupposes a fair degree of insight, especially if one is to say it with equanimity. All the same, whether he can talk intelligently about it or not, that pupil is under pressure, not necessarily because someone has done this to him, but because it happened automatically, as we spoke of it earlier, entirely on account of the presence of an adult who has certain knowledge. We differentiate between incidental and intentional pressure. This is important, for various reasons. The incidental pressure is not caused by the teacher, nor by the comparatively greater knowledge of the teacher. The pupil may, after a time, suppose the pressure he experiences is in fact caused by the teacher or by something to do with the teacher, and if he does so he is simply wrong. There is no need, however, to make an issue of this. The important thing for the teacher to recognize is that the pupil cannot help but feel somehow burdened due to his, the mature teacher's, worthwhile presence as someone with certain knowledge. If no such burden is felt by the pupil, no real teaching or learning can go on. Either this adult has nothing to offer or else he has not yet begun to offer it.

To suppose, therefore, that one can teach in a way so that the pupil experiences no pressure and feels no load, no inconvenience or discomfort, is self-delusion. There are those who would teach by play and while having fun rather than risking any pressure, but this is an impossibility. Fun and games may come into it but in no way can they substitute for, or do away with, the pressure-burden of which a pupil becomes somehow conscious, even though it may be some time before he actually becomes aware of it.

Besides, it would be quite wrong of a teacher to try to avoid or forestall this incidental pressure or burden. After all, what else can happen when the pupil first begins to sense this certain knowledge? To him it must be entirely new. In comparison to what the pupil has, this knowledge is both greater and different.

The pupil's sense apparatus will have to improve, to grow. His capacity for thinking and feeling has to be extended. He may not even know yet that what he wants is precisely what the teacher has on offer. Naturally he feels depressed, taken aback, cowed – even if only slightly. But even this slight set-back in the pupil has to be accounted for by the teacher, somehow, by some aspect of what he means by pedagogy. We are not making a mountain out of a molehill here. If this business of incidental, uncaused pressure, of a load that suddenly happens to be there, is not properly and generously understood, the teacher builds on unsound foundations.

We repeat: the burden is not caused by the teacher nor by his certain knowledge. It is not caused by anything. It is, simply, the pupil's inertia since he is a prospective learner. It has nothing to do with laziness, with stubbornness or stupidity. Not initially. These may somehow get mixed up with it due to various misunderstandings and malpractices, but initially the load incidentally felt by a pupil in the presence of a teacher with certain knowledge on offer is unavoidable inertia, as mechanical and necessary as the falling of a stone off a ledge in England.

*

Earlier we said that every human being, whether he knows it or not, wants to grow, to learn; to move from one state into another.

We have isolated something now that happens automatically when a teacher confronts a pupil in a prospective teaching-learning situation. The pupil begins to experience his own inertia. This inertia is not something that exists in the pupil prior to this situation but comes along with it. We are interested here in a relative pupil, not in 'the absolute pupil'.

What does exist in the pupil prior to his becoming a pupil is a want to be educated; to be shown, to be more and more included in the adult world. It would be fine if parents, and all parental adults in a child's vicinity, were always to keep in mind that child's want to grow up and then to grow, like those adults. But alas! We grown-ups are much more in the habit of ignoring that child's individual want and instead burdening him with dogma. Dogma, where we transfer finished products, compared to subjectivism, where we 'leave it to the child' and only 'surround him with choices', is only the other side of the same false coin.

So here is something that every teacher has to take into account. Let's call it the falsification of expectations. Due to their want to be educated, and at the same time on account, frequently, of the lack of such education from day to day, the child ends up with stones instead of bread. He imagines for himself what it might be that he wants and naturally comes up with some unsuitable conclusions, and, from the other side, he is spoiled or perverted by dogma and delusion, neither of which satisfies his want to be educated. The same goes, of course, for immature adults.

The teacher can be seen now to be confronting a pupil who not only feels the pressure of his inertia but who in addition to this is bound to reflect on some degree, however slight, of actual pain due to a force he experiences.

We are looking, now, at what happens to the pupil in the face of certain knowledge not on account of his own less certain or uncertain knowledge, but on account of his *spoiled and perverted faculties*. What he experiences there is a force, or the sensation of being forced. Force is different from pressure. Pressure I experience on myself, force on my faculties. We say that our faculties are perverted when they are dissuaded from their true function. So we need to have some notion that there is such a thing as the true function of human faculties. These faculties are spoiled, in turn, if they do not so much function wrongly, however energetically, but poorly or not at all.

There is not much need for the teacher to analyze what has gone wrong or why it has gone wrong. Some obvious malpractices or bad habits may have to be carefully countenanced, but much more important is it that the teacher remain aware, and first of all, of course, become aware, of the fact that the pupil, in the presence of certain knowledge, feels forced, and that this is painful for him. The pressure, as we discussed earlier, is inconvenient, uncomfortable, and the pupil is liable to feel, or even be, miserable; but the force, the sense of this force, is actually painful and so the pupil flinches and shrinks.

Again, one wonders how education can possibly take place.

But it does take place, as soon as the teacher, in the case of the inconvenient pressure and misery, extends compassion to the pupil, and then, in the case of the pain, as soon as he suffers for the pupil.

*

Surely this is too much to ask of a teacher? Compassion, yes. But suffering? What sort of person is a teacher, that we should ask such a thing of him? Certainly he must be an exceptional person. Here he can tell that a pupil is secretly in pain, and so he does something about it. He does not inwardly say to the pupil: "I hate you because you do not accept and reach for my knowledge with outstretched arms but instead you wince and demonstrate unwillingness", but he says: "I am not surprised that you flinch when I approach you. I myself do that when confronted by my own teacher; and when I turn to him and excuse myself for behaving in ignorance or for having behaved hatefully when I was confronted by new experience, he never holds it against me. Neither will I hold your demonstration of antipathy against you. You don't know what you are doing, but then I am the teacher and am I not here to help you find out what you are doing? Should I condemn you for behaving like a pupil? No, I will excuse you as I myself usually get excused. I will pardon as I am pardoned. When I experienced resistance, I interpreted this as you under pressure and my heart went out to you. Now I experience antipathy, even hatred, and I interpret this in a similar fashion, to mean that you feel antipathy and hatred towards me, not because you choose to do so, but because it happens to you. Probably you have no notion of it as such. If I were to ask if you hated me, you would very likely deny it. But I can tell that you hate me, by the hate I experience in myself. Since I am a teacher, I am sensitive in this way. Should I try to make you agree with me about this? Not at all. It remains unimportant to me, whether or not you know that you hate both me and the knowledge I offer. Yes, you actually hate the knowledge I offer, even though you do in yourself want to be educated to precisely such knowledge. No need, however, for you to believe or accept this. I can do something so that this mechanical hatred of yours is simply annihilated. Would it not be much better, then, if I just went ahead and did that, and forgot all about enlightening you as to this revulsion you feel? Of course it would. I feel the revulsion myself, this revulsion of yours. It seems for all the world like my own. I'll tell you what. Instead of explaining to you that you accidentally hate, and instead of justifying myself in my own eyes by reminding myself that this hatred does not, after all, originate with me, I will go ahead and inwardly behave exactly as though this were my own hatred. I will take the responsibility for it. Is it not my dearest wish that you should be rid of this revulsion and learn? Did no one suffer my own revulsion when my opportunity came to take on the certain knowledge which I extend to you now? I know fine well that my own learning is frequently interrupted by my various bad habits of rebelliousness. Here now I have been given the golden opportunity to be ashamed of myself on your behalf. I do it with gratitude.

*

Let's be clear about one thing: no such hatred is felt by a teacher who adheres to a standard. Only in the case of creative education, where children themselves, as whole beings, are considered, can it happen, first of all, that the wrongness and badness of certain faculties in the child are actually challenged, and then, that the teacher can experience the hatred which is automatically transferred to him from the child. We are not speaking of dislike, nor even of intense dislike, which crops up during standard education and interrupts the smooth functioning of a mechanical process, but of actual hatred, which can be described as a desire to annihilate and destroy. The teacher is on the lookout for it and knows what to do. He has discussed this with other teachers and although he too flinches at first, he then interprets it as a golden opportunity. He must not allow himself to get in the habit of pretending that hatred is dislike, even intense dislike, in the hope that a few kind words, a few lies and moralistic compromises, can remedy the situation and bring things back to normal. A creative teacher never tries to get back to normal. He knows no standard of normality, no desirable harmony of mere appearances.

What could, after all, be more exciting for a human being – indeed, what could be more human – than to suffer the pain of another and turn hatred into love!

One hesitates to speak of love in the case of education but it seems it cannot be avoided. One hesitates to speak of love under any circumstances because of the modern confusion with sexuality on one side and with romantic feelings on the other. But the love we mean here cannot avoid an association in our minds with pain on one side and with hatred on the other.

Let's not forget that the opportunity for this uniquely human love, which is so different from popular love, arises within the context of faculties and their functioning, in other words much more in terms of our doing than our being. This is not to minimize what goes on in the case of resistance, pressure and compassion, where being is more in the forefront than doing. All the same we do well to distinguish between the two, between being miserable, for example, and hating.

We have come around now to the position where we feel obliged to acknowledge that a creative teacher, when he is miserable, can turn this misery into compassion, and when he hates, can turn this hatred into love. Here we have arrived at the very heart of creative education. All its successes and all its failures may be explained or diagnosed from here. And as we saw, it depends on the teacher being sensitive and open to the pupil in a most definite way. The difference between the standard teacher and a creative teacher is nowhere more obvious. In order to highlight this difference we might speak of creative temperament and of creative imagination.

*

To what sort of a person might it occur to undertake creative education and to become a creative teacher? If we mention just those two, creative imagination and temperament, we open the discussion towards some understanding, at least, of what it is in someone that makes such education both desirable and possible.

Can we, for example, imagine human being as something quite out of the ordinary, in comparison to all other being? Do we feel the need to imagine human being as essential to all other life forms? If we do, then our imagining faculty does more than represent for us what is. It reminds us of what might be and has never been before. The sense of the totally new clings to it. Such an experience – and we must call it an experience, though we mean an experience of our own imagination – would prove disconcertingly fruitless if we were tantalized by glorious possibilities but lacked the power and the faculties to realize them. Which is why we right away draw to our aid what we can call creative temperament.

Temperament isolates. It allows us to take issue with one thing at a time, to apply ourselves to one problem at a time. Without it we flit from one moment to the next without coming to grips with a task. So temperament in itself is good because without it we cannot be really effective.

But the difference between just plain temperament and creative temperament is crucial. It makes little difference, now, whether we regard creative temperament as some special gift with which some are endowed and for which many might ask, or whether we regard just plain temperament as what is left when the creativity has gone out of creative temperament, through malfunction and neglect. The main point at issue here is how we behave during a crisis. Either we happen to resent the hardship of the crisis and then indulge our resentment, so as to get things back to normal, back to the standard, or else we happen to resent the hardship and then encounter our resentment, in awareness of its meaning. It is our awareness, of this unintentional resentment as being meaningful, that characterizes creative temperament.

The resentment, however little, sets in with the hardship and as the hardship of a crisis, when things do not go as we expected them to go, as we planned, or as we had hoped. If we indulge our resentment, we do something bad and bring evil into the world and prepare a woeful experience for ourselves later. In order not to indulge in the unavoidable resentment, we have to encounter it awarely as meaningful. What could it mean? As we experience the hardship, we might ask ourselves: what could this possibly mean, this frustration, this crippling influence on my will, this judgment upon me? The question is quite usual, during a crisis, and while we ask what it might mean, we receive no answer. In this or that sense the crisis is meaningless, and we ourselves in that crisis feel worthless and impotent. Anyone who works with other human beings is perhaps especially familiar with such critical experience.

The point is, that the resentment means neither this nor that, but it is in itself meaningful. This is to be understood in the following way. If dark clouds in the sky <u>mean</u> imminent rain and thunder, then for us, who are aware of that meaning, a progression of understanding and a conclusion from a present to a future state becomes possible and is drawn. Some uncertainty always exists however. A type of scientific investigation tries to remove all such uncertainty by discovering the one most meaningful law, but must of course fail. The complete certainty is not achieved for me until not my understanding alone, nor any part of me alone, but I myself progress from this state to the next. Invariably the popular imagination always moves that next state beyond the grave. A creative person however himself moves always and again into that new state. And encountering critical resentment in oneself as meaningful in itself is in fact such a move. Meaningful here means something like: capable of transporting into perfect reality, or: affording passage into true reality. All that remains for me to do, in the case of experienced resentment, so that the move will actually take place, is to know and believe that the resentment, while I hold out in the face of it, is in fact meaningful in this way. Not that the resentment itself transports. Ignorant resentment amounts right away to harmful indulgence. It's my awareness of the resentment and of the entire resentful experience as meaningful that allows me to hold out – while I am usefully changed. The change from this state to the next has to be instigated for me, as something that happens; I cannot instigate it myself. The change I myself can instigate is the change to something other than myself. A creative person knows that he himself is to undergo change, and this has to come upon him, rather than being brought about by him. His own part is to comply, and he can do this with a degree or more of intelligence. The most intelligent compliance is also the least painful and least onerous one, and it is an awareness of what we should perhaps call 'crucial', not 'critical' resentment as simply meaningful towards reality.

Creative temperament then might be described as my realization of meaningful resentment during a crisis.

We can see now how imagination and temperament, if creative, work hand in hand. Via imagination we discover the good that is possible and by means of temperament we receive it and make it ours. Imaginatively I learn what eternal life, for example, is all about, and temperamentally I manage to weather the crisis, or crises, so that I may live and not die.

We do not hop, skip and trick ourselves into human value, but we grow into it. Such growth is the essence of life for any creative teacher. He understands education in reference to it.

*

So when we ask: What sort of a person can be a creative teacher? – we have to keep in mind this capacity and willingness to weather a crisis productively. What we said about the educational process relates to this of course. The resistance or dislike turned into compassion, the hate turned into a loving sufferance, in the knowledge of how similar experiences arise in a pupil: such activity is crucial to the creative educational process. But now we moved for a time away from the teacher-pupil interaction in order to contemplate what we might call the creative personality of the teacher himself, outside the classroom.

Someone for whom pain is meaningless cannot teach. Pain is involved during the reception of certain knowledge. Learning cannot be separated from pain. Therefore those for whom pain is only a setback and a totally negative experience cannot begin to teach anything. A person who would teach must know something in his or her own life of the critical and crucial experience inseparable from real growth, and he must be in the habit of associating growth with learning. Learning will mean to him something like the establishment of a human connection, and he will recognize in himself a yearning for this connection just as he will acknowledge a predisposition for such a connection literally in everything. He distinguishes between, on one hand, learning information and skills, which he does not neglect, and, on the other hand, the learning of beauty, truth and reality, which he actively pursues.

*

Nothing sounds more absurd than 'the learning of beauty, truth and reality' to someone who sees learning exclusively in terms of data information and skills for survival. From the standpoint of survival such things as beauty, truth and reality mean something entirely different, if they mean anything at all. A creative person, whose point of vantage is not survival but life, can readily associate beauty and terror, pain with the truth and death with reality, but by terror, pain and death he means things that lead him to a variety of options. He is never afraid of them for very long, though he might momentarily chide himself for having once again been afraid. He flinches – and gets on with it.

Really all we are saying here is that someone who would teach creatively is bound to be a creative person. Not every creative person is a teacher, but something of creativity rubs off whatever one's calling.

A discussion of the creative teacher can therefore justifiably commence with an appreciation of the creative personality. There are certain activities such a teacher leaves behind in the classroom, but these education activities can usefully be seen as adaptations of ordinary personal activities to the specific task of teaching.

Again, it would be unfair to a non-creative individual and to people in general if one insisted that what was ordinary and even normal for a creative person must be so also for them. The creative person would be the first to admit how privileged he is in being able to see, to think and feel, in a way that is life furthering, and it would never enter his head to chide others, who cannot see, for not being able to see. Though he might chide those who insist that only a decent look is possible.

So now here we come around to an attitude that will be found in almost every creative person who seriously contemplates the activity rightly called teaching. It is an attitude towards non-creative individuality. It is an attitude a prospective teacher would establish and practice. Especially the practice of it appeals to him. He would go so far as to call it 'the practical attitude'. It is an attitude especially useful to him during both the development and exercise of his skills as a teacher. (Life skills, not survival skills, and to be understood specifically with regard to what we elsewhere called creative transformation.) To a prospective teacher this attitude would seem very congenial, and to the extent that it appeals to him, he will entertain the notion of becoming and being a teacher.

What does he understand by this practical attitude so dear to his heart? He might describe it as a cheerful openness to all individuality not yet become personal.

Really we mean something here that pertains to a prospective teacher's most common relation to all human beings, and to all human being, not just to pupils. We are talking about the way someone might go about asking himself: 'Shall I teach?' We mean that his question might readily take the form of: 'What is my attitude towards individuality not yet become personal? Does it matter to me if someone finds it difficult to communicate? Does my heart go out to those who seem stuck in their individuality, to those who have not yet experienced the joy of human relationship? Does it anger me if I have addressed someone who seemed to me perfectly capable of perception but he refuses to respond? Does it anger me or do I remain indifferent and turn elsewhere for a response?'

The one who answers: 'Yes, it does matter to me and I pity those who are trapped in their individuality rather than being propelled by it and it does make me angry that perception should be possible but not entertained,' would then be smart to ask himself: 'In that case, how do I feel about allowing this attitude to turn into an actual disposition in my case? I find that this attitude is frequently and readily my own, and gladly do I support it in others, but in order to teach, although this attitude is essential, more is required. In order effectively to teach creatively I must be willing that such an attitude as this should not remain an attitude, but that I would behave in accordance with it, under given circumstances. Am I willing to act, on the basis and in line with the motivation implied by this attitude? It's one thing that something should matter to me and make a difference to me, but it is something additional for me to do something about it. I might walk past the beggar indifferent. I might deplore his plight. Then I still have to put my hand in my pocket.'

There is something in that comparison of the individual to the beggar, and of the good Samaritan to the teacher, but let's not make too much of it. Creative teaching is also a specific application of certain character traits. For an attitude to become a disposition, a definite predilection must be acquired for a certain way of doing things. It might, on the surface, suffice that one does these things often enough until they become routine. A sense of duty, diligence, self-discipline and a healthy respect for the pay-cheque at the end of the month – all these support a respectable routine, based on an attitude. However a disposition is not a routine, and for a disposition to – take root and grow! – a sense of duty and financial reward cannot suffice. Disposition implies alacrity, celerity and zeal. 'Could I possibly come up with these?' asks the prospective teacher. He must ask himself. It will hardly do if another asks him. 'Might I be disposed to teach in this way?' he asks. 'Let me see if I can get a taste for it, if I don't have one yet.'

So he places himself under such conditions as might be conducive. Special conditions can be created so that those who might one day teach can test themselves. The creation of such conditions is a topic all its own.

Suffice it to be said here, that some of those who are willing to find out if they might in fact let their attitude towards individuality and individuals become a disposition will in fact discover in themselves – or have revealed to them in themselves – a predisposition. As soon as they do, they know they are cut out to be teachers.

*

Let's not make too much, at this stage, of the ways and means by which someone can find out if creative teaching is for him. But we must hold fast to that attitude towards individuality and its tendency towards, or away from, personality, because no doctrine of education can dispense with that. A teacher will look at a pupil and discern. Always his own inner being is the system of apperception. The teacher picks up the vibrations, if you like, of individuality from the pupil by way of his own inner being, so that for the time being his own individuality is highlighted, and in a way that would lead him to suppose, if he were ignorant, that he is learning something about himself and that he might judge the pupil as the cause of it. If the teacher once again feels 'encouraged' by John's progress in algebra, does he praise John? If he 'feels in despair', suddenly, over John's lack of progress, does he chide him? But John's progress or lack of progress in algebra should never become an issue. It should never be moved into the foreground, where praise or blame might attach to John on account of it. The teacher's 'feelings of encouragement or despair' do not, in fact, mean that, and should not mean that to the teacher. The teacher has to take care that they do not come to mean that to him. If they do, he has mistaken the pupil's individuality and he has misled the child. We all know from personal experience how praise does not necessarily please us and how blame at times leaves us absolutely indifferent. I can still remember how it sickened me to be paraded, as a child, in front of my own class and other classes because I had acquired the knack for singing at sight from sheet music. I could tell that something was going wrong inside me, on account of this 'prize' I was being handed. It made me vain, in spite of my own, albeit still dim, better judgment. When one day I refused, out of sheer 'rebellious-ness', as it would have been called, against the standard which was called my standard but which had been foisted on me by a well-meaning standard teacher, I was shamed in front of the class. Both the ridicule and the applause damaged me, set me apart, made it more difficult for me to relate to others in a way that would have been genuine and personal for me. The cause of this was that the teacher had not dealt with his feelings crea-tively. He had allowed the 'encouragement' and the 'disap-pointment' to mislead him, in what was after all a quite stand-ard way. When he felt the 'encouragement', that should have meant to him: This pupil is presently finding something easy; perhaps I could give him some more to do. When he felt the 'despair' about me, that should have meant to him: This pupil is presently having trouble with something. Let me above all extend my sympathy. – Why should someone be blamed for being in trouble?

Earlier on we spoke of the mix of individualities. What the teacher experienced as joy and as despair was indeed such a mix, such a chaos of sensations and opinions. Then why did it seem perfectly clear to him, as I assume it did, that I should be, respectively, applauded and accused? What was missing in him, that he could not distance himself from this chaos but he remained prejudicially entangled in it, making wrong decisions in bad faith?

He was simply not aware of himself as a creative teacher. He was not aware of his individuality as of something to be used to discover the present state of being of his pupil. There were other times when he probably did behave creatively, but on that instance, which I cite as an example of the standard approach in comparison to the creative one, he behaved uncreatively and caused mischief – though no doubt he meant well and did only what most other teachers at the time in that place would have found quite laudable.

He lacked an awareness of his individuality. He lacked, on that occasion, a creative attitude.

So first of all, I suppose we might say, we must develop such a thing as an attitude towards our individual inner being. It's like being properly awake. If we ourselves are not awake, how can we possibly awaken others? Children are to be awakened to the freedom of adulthood. By whom?

Our attitude, as teachers now, must include: primarily the knowledge of any human being's want to be educated, of his still unconscious or perhaps semi-conscious, inborn urge to grow up and be responsible as a free human being in personal relation to others; and secondarily it must include an understanding of what we might call particular human beings' present state of mortification. This we have described in terms of faculties that do not properly, or not at all, function.

*

Our consideration of that inborn want to be educated applies generally, and we keep it in mind as we appreciate and approve of any pupil's individuality. But what we called the state of mortification is particular, not general. Seen in a general light, why can that want to be educated not always be entirely satisfied by a parent and teacher, so that no mortification happens? Or why, once a state of mortification has been identified, in some particular pupil's case, can it not simply be remedied? Why should we not regard all human being in a general light and reject everything particular as a disturbance, as so many systems of education undertake to do?

The answer is, of course, that not all of a human being can be seen in a general light. The cyclopean approach is detrimental, whether from the general or the particular aspect. We distinguish between being and doing, between mind and body, between the general and the particular, and so on, for the same reason that we distinguish between our right and left eye, our right and left hand, etc.

A doctrine of education, then, would do well to draw our attention equally to both the general and the particular, and we try to keep in mind that neither can be complete on its own.

Gradually our educational attitude, if we have decided to become teachers, becomes more differentiated and more articulate, our points of view become more numerous and each one more informed due to practical experience in the light of theoretic vision and knowledge.

But we have hardly yet begun to make use of the various possibilities of insight to be gained along these two lines of enquiry. Therefore we consider this to be a good point of departure for our actual doctrine of creative education.

* * *

36

www.ingramcontent.com/pod-product-compliance
Lightning Source LLC
Chambersburg PA
CBHW070348290526
45791CB00003B/1486